MW01601061

The Young Christian Professionals Workbook

1st Edition

ISBN#979-8-9875230-0-1

Visit us at: www.YoungChristianProfessionals.org
IG @ycpleadership
FB: https://www.facebook.com/YCPLeadership
email: ycpgodlyleadership@gmail.com

ODRC Director, Annette Chambers-Smith, at Richland prison commending its then-incarcerated co-founder and presenting Y.C.P. Staff Advisors with Impact Awards for Oustanding Program (October 2019)

The Students

" I found myself looking forward to the days I got to go to class. I learned a lot and enjoyed the teachings!"
~ R. Daniels, Y.C.P. Graduate

" Y.C.P. has helped me put my life goals in perspective."
~ J. Bradley, Y.C.P. Graduate

" I learned to better the relationship with my children's mother, and so far it's been working!"
~ PJ, Y.C.P. Graduate

" It helped me get into a different way of thinking. Certain situations I looked at differently because of what Y.C.P has taught me."
~ M. Cawthon, Y.C.P. Graduate

Table of Contents

Introduction

Welcome to Y.C.P.! We are honored to have you as part of our inspired program!

The Young Christian Professionals' curriculum and workbook is designed to develop leaders into the image of Christ-likeness through its powerful 4-component program which includes:

- **8 Biblical Character Development studies** *(The Classroom)*

- **8 Executive Etiquette Trainings** *(The Boardroom),* which also includes Personal Testimonies from Christian business owners and execs

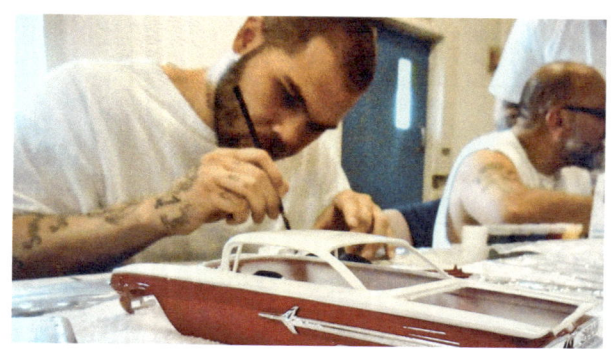

- **VirtueCraft** (optional), a therapeutic arts & crafts workshop session promoting patience and other virtues. *(Contact our website for information on our Model Car and Basket Weaving programs)*

- **Inspi-Reading** (optional) *The Brand Within* by Daymond John is our dynamic reading collaboration as a supplemental option for those who wish to empower their participants with an understanding of how their own conduct and integrity is their brand!

Uniqueness

The uniqueness of our ministry is that it is created to address the specific needs of our youth today while encouraging wisdom from its mature participants and setting our group on a course for success in both their personal and vocational lives.

We hope you enjoy the program, the studies, and the activities! We will be standing in the gap, praying fervently for you as you embark on this wonderful journey of growth and leadership right before your very own eyes!

God bless you all, and remember, Y.C.P. is not the business world invading the church, but the church invading the business world!

Mission Statement:

The mission of Y.C.P. is to
develop and dispatch godly leaders

Overview

The following is a summary of the 8-week studies contained herein:

WEEK ONE
ORIENTATION
"What is Y.C.P?" page and Y.C.P. Creed review takes place here. Commitment Sheets and Questionaires will also be handed out, explained and signed here as well.

WEEK TWO
Lesson: **EXCUSES**
Boardroom: A YOUNG CHRISTIAN PROFESSIONAL

WEEK THREE
Lesson: **ATTITUDE**
Boardroom: YOUNG LADIES AND GENTLEMEN

WEEK FOUR
Lesson: **PURPOSE**
Boardroom: THE POLISHED YOUNG MAN AND WOMAN

WEEK FIVE
Lesson: **YOUR POWER TEAM**
Boardroom: HOW TO STAY FOCUSED IN A CHAOTIC ENVIRONMENT

WEEK SIX
Lesson: **TURNING FEAR TO FAITH**
Boardroom: RELATIONAL POLISH

WEEK SEVEN
Lesson: **THE KEYS**
Boardroom: SERVANT LEADERSHIP

WEEK EIGHT
Lesson: **TRUSTING GOD**
Boardroom: THE PROFESSIONAL

WEEK ONE:
ORIENTATION

"Developing and Dispatching Godly Leaders"

Week 1: Orientation
(Psalms 15)

THIS WEEK'S CHALLENGES:

Check below
once completed

☐ **Start Proverbs reading plan** (read one chapter in the book of Proverbs a day, beginning with that particular day of week; write insights, convictions and application in your journal

☐ **Complete Section 1, Lesson 1, in "A Man Called Jesus" book**

Optional:

☐ Read Introduction & Chapter 1 of "The Brand Within" and complete attached handout

---

What is Y.C.P.?

Young Christian Professionals (Y.C.P.) is an organization taking a proactive stand against crime, drugs, gangs, and poverty, by reaching out to the youth with the most powerful weapon known to man...love!

With godly instructors who have experienced the abounding love of Jesus, we extend that love systematically through a comprehensive 4-component program which includes: Biblical Character Development studies, Executive Etiquette Trainings (which includes personal testimonies from Christian business owners), an optional therapeutic Arts & Crafts workshop and optional Reading component.

Created by 3 former inmates with over 50 years prison experience combined, the men understood the specific needs of today's young people and joined forces to address their needs right where they were in a way that would be exciting, fun, and practical.

The curriculum is a 8-week course requiring participation in its primary classes. The **Character Development Study**, which is taught through the first 30 minutes, serves to empower participants in finding purpose, gaining integrity, and building a relationship with Jesus Christ. The second portion of the class, **The Boardroom**, is where Executive Etiquette Training takes place which aims to instill personal and executive manners, professionalism, and respect. Periodically throughout the 8-week tenure, we invite a Christian businessman or businesswoman in to share how Biblical character has impacted their work and business life.

Additionally, it is the Young Christian Professional's aim to develop leaders, particularly those returning to society, and empower them to impact their communities and workplaces to the glory of God.

Y.C.P. CREED

- Jesus is my Lord and King;
  He is my real boss. (Col. 3:23)

- I am a representative of the King, (2Cor. 5:20)
  and will carry myself as such.

- I will extend the same love to others
  that He has extended to me. (Jn. 13:34)

- I will not be on time, but early,
  for being early is on time. (Psalms 63:1)

- I will conduct all of my business with integrity,
  honesty, and fairness. (Psalms 15:2)

- I will not lie to anyone for any reason (Col. 3:9)
  and will suffer the penalty for truth.

- I will conduct myself with professionalism
  and keep my word by all means. (Mt. 5: 37)

- I think more highly of others than myself (Phil. 2:3)
  and value all of my relationships.

- I will be a light and example to my family, friends, and all whom I
  work with; (Mt. 5:16) and will follow through on whatever I start.

- I will not look back and allow the past to hinder my future in Christ
  Jesus. (Phil. 3:13-14; Lk. 9: 62)

PROVERBS READING PLAN

Read a chapter of Proverbs each day of the week that corresponds to the day of the month it is. Write your insights below from a particular verse in that chapter.

Chapter_____Verse_____

Insight: _____

_____

_____

_____

Chapter_____Verse_____

Insight: _____

_____

_____

_____

Chapter_____Verse_____

Insight: _____

_____

_____

_____

Chapter_____Verse_____

Insight: _____

_____

_____

_____

Chapter_____Verse_____

Insight: _____

_____

_____

_____

Chapter_____Verse_____

Insight: _____

_____

_____

_____

Chapter_____Verse_____

Insight: _____

_____

_____

_____

WEEK TWO:
EXCUSES

"Developing and Dispatching Godly Leaders"

Week 2: EXCUSES

THIS WEEK'S CHALLENGES:

Check below
once completed

☐   Continue Proverbs reading plan

☐   Complete Section 1, Lesson 2 in "A Man Called Jesus" book (pgs. 10-14)

☐   **Challenge:** Write out 30 things about yourself.

Optional:

☐   Read Chapter 2 in "The Brand Within" and complete attached handout

---

Week 2:
Excuses
(Luke 14: 15-24)

Read Luke 14: 15-24 together

1. Does you know anyone who makes a lot of excuses?

2. How does it feel when you hear excuses?

3. What were the excuses made by the "A-list" guests to the man who prepared the great feast? What is the problem with these excuses?

- **"I have just bought a field and must inspect it."**

- **"I have just bought five pairs of oxen, and I want to try them out. Please excuse me."**

- **"I now have a wife, so I can't come"**

Overall excuse?_____

The people invited first allow everyday concerns to overwhelm them from the need to celebrate life. It is a matter of one's priorities and values. This parable demonstrates how some people are just hearers of the word and miss the opportunity for a seat at the mighty table of salvation now extended to all people.

What is the Gentile Inclusion? In response to the Jews refusing to enter, the Gentiles are now welcomed into the Kingdom of God as the host switches plans after his first set of guests give excuses not to come to the party. He replaces these unwilling guests with B-list guests—people from the streets, then invites people on the fringes, the poor, the blind and the lame. These guests are not people he was normally around. They were outsiders.

Why else do we make excuses?

What is keeping you from being the best version of you?

Read Lamentations 3: 22-24
Every day is a new day in which we can move in a direction that defines our eternity.

The Young Christian Professional does all he can to avoid making excuses!

WEEK TWO:
THE BOARDROOM

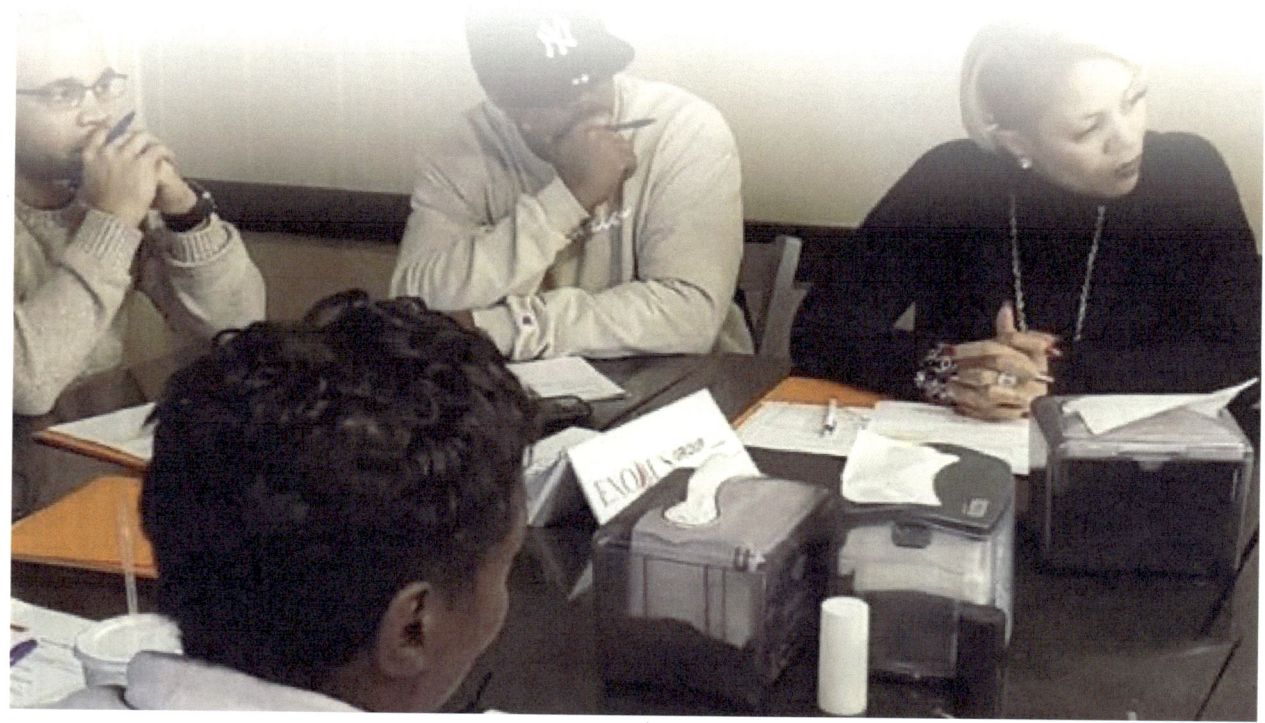

Week 2:
A Young
Christian Professional

- Doesn't lie, and keeps their word

- Returns calls, emails and texts promptly

- Practices what they preach. They do not expect others to follow rules they do not follow themselves

- Begins meetings on time. If not, you'll lose the overachievers of the group

- Gives credit where credit is due

- Criticizes in private, and even then, does so constructively

- Sends memos to all who are working on a project together so egos are not bruised

- Is sympathetic to those they works with, especially when family misfortunes befall them

- Does not act like they know everything when they don't

- Does not brag or boast

- Takes time out for those new to the group, and helps them adjust

- Considers all ideas valuable

- Stands up for their employees

- Listens to those under them, as well as gives them orders

- Draws attention to those who worked hard behind the scenes

PROVERBS READING PLAN

Read a chapter of Proverbs each day of the week that corresponds to the day of the month it is. Write your insights below from a particular verse in that chapter.

Chapter_____Verse_____

Insight: _____

_____

_____

_____

Chapter_____Verse_____

Insight: _____

_____

_____

_____

Chapter_____Verse_____

Insight: _____

_____

_____

_____

Chapter_____Verse_____

Insight: _____

_____

_____

_____

Chapter_____Verse_____

Insight: _____

_____

_____

_____

Chapter_____Verse_____

Insight: _____

_____

_____

_____

Chapter_____Verse_____

Insight: _____

_____

_____

_____

Challenge

Challenge

_____

_____

_____

_____

_____

_____

_____

_____

_____

_____

_____

_____

_____

_____

_____

_____

_____

_____

_____

_____

_____

_____

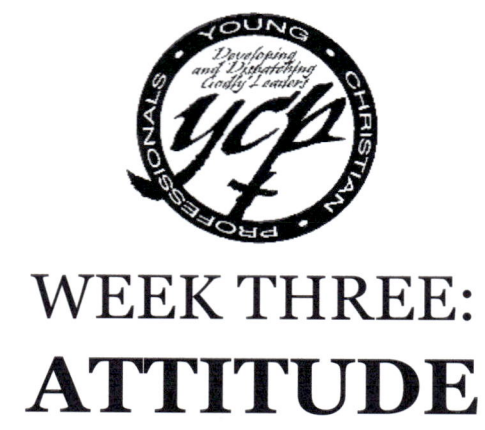

WEEK THREE:
ATTITUDE

"Developing and Dispatching Godly Leaders"

Week 3: Attitude
THIS WEEK'S CHALLENGES:

Check below
once completed

☐ Continue Proverbs reading plan

☐ Complete Section 1, Lesson 3 in "A Man Called Jesus" book (pgs. 15-19)

☐ Write out some examples of when you had a good attitude and bad attitude.

Optional:

☐ Read Chapter 3 in "The Brand Within" and complete attached handout

Week 3:
ATTITUDE

1. What is Attitude?

2. How are attitudes formed?

3. What results from our attitudes?

** Read Genesis 4 together

4. Why did Cain kill Abel?

5. Why did God accept Abel's sacrifice over Cain's?

6. How did it make Cain feel?

7. After the murder, what kind of attitude did Cain exhibit, (4: 9) good or bad? Towards who?

8. What do you have an attitude with God about?

** Read 2Samuel 12: 1-14

8. What was David's response to sin?

9. What does that look like? (Psalms 51)

Romans 6: 23
"For the wages of sin is death; but the gift of God is eternal life through Jesus Christ our lord."

1John 1: 8-10
"If we say that we have no sin, we deceive ourselves, and the truth is not in us. If we confess our sins, He is faithful and just to forgive us our sins, and to cleanse us from all unrighteousness. If we say that we have not sinned, we make Him a liar, and His word is not in us."

10. What should be our response to sin?

Group Attitudes

In the early part of the twentieth century, several hundred thousand Japanese immigrants rushed to the mainland United States, especially to California. This immigration brought about the first massive encounter between Americans and Japanese, and resulted in the rise of anti-Japanese movements. Although the government played some role in these movements, the major actors were private organizations and white men who needed work and felt threatened by job loss. Attitudes against Japanese people changed for the worse which forced the laws to change, virtually shutting Japanese immigration down around that time

These group attitudes change and shift from group to group at various times. Around 9/11, attitudes towards Middle-Eastern people changed for the worse. In the early 90's, attitudes towards the incarcerated changed as people felt threatened by job loss and the education inmates were receiving while incarcerated and a 1994 bill was enacted that stopped it.

Do you have any prejudices against any groups?_____

Attitudes Towards Work (Na'im Akbar, 1984))

One of the attitudes which has been passed to African-Americans is their rather distorted attitude towards work. Slavery was forced labor. Kenneth Stamp (1956) described the work of the slave occurring 'from day clear to first dark.' The day's toil would begin just before sunrise and would end at dusk. Work would begin in early childhood and continuing until death or total disability.

The slave was forced to work under the threat of abuse or even death, but the work was not for the purpose of providing for his life's needs. Instead, he worked to produce for the slave owners. He would not profit from his labor, instead it improved the life of the owners.

*Work, in a natural society, is looked upon with pride, both because it permits people to express themselves and because it supplies their survival needs. During slavery, work was used as punishment. Work became hated, as does any activity which causes suffering and brings no rewards for the doer. **Work became equated with slavery**. Even today, the African-American slang expression which refers to a job as a 'slave' communicates the painful connection. (For example, "They're working me like a Hebrew slave!)*

Despite the fact that we are over one hundred years removed from the direct slavery experience, African-Americans still to a great extent hate work. Work was identified as the activity for the underdog and was difficult to be viewed with pride. Work is something approached unwillingly and out of necessity only. The ability to look successful without doing any identifiable work became the image of affluence of many street hustlers and pimps.

WEEK THREE:
THE BOARDROOM

Week 3:
Young Ladies & Gentlemen

"After you, is good manners."

- They are hospitable
- He always carries packages and opens doors for a woman
- She's always gracious and attentive to those around her
- He never disrespects or puts his hands on a woman
- They are always considerate to loners in a group
- She's refined, polite and well-spoken
- Never brings someone to an event without calling first and receiving permission
- Is on time. If they can't make it they call the host and inform them
- Doesn't talk about invites around those who haven't been invited
- Is always considerate of guests at an event, even when it's not theirs
- Helps the host of an event whenever needed
- Is never aggressive or too pushy concerning being invited
- Knows how to introduce people properly
- Always respects the rituals and customs of the group (church, synagogue etc.) they've been invited to attend. If too uncomfortable, don't attend
- Never repeats a rumor that would hurt someone's rep
- Always gives people their property back when they borrow it!
- Picks up the check at the restaurant or bar when it is their turn
- Compliments appropriately and knows how to accept compliments with grace as well
- Dresses the part and looks adequate to the setting
- Writes personal letters or texts when they find out news of others' good fortune (such as promotions, accomplishments etc.)
- They do their best to avoid arguments or violence

PROVERBS READING PLAN

Read a chapter of Proverbs each day of the week that corresponds to the day of the month it is. Write your insights below from a particular verse in that chapter.

Chapter_____Verse_____

Insight: _____

_____

_____

_____

Chapter_____Verse_____

Insight: _____

_____

_____

_____

Chapter_____Verse_____

Insight: _____

_____

_____

_____

Chapter_____Verse_____

Insight: _____

_____

_____

_____

Chapter_____Verse_____

Insight: _____

_____

_____

_____

Chapter_____Verse_____

Insight: _____

_____

_____

_____

Chapter_____Verse_____

Insight: _____

_____

_____

_____

Challenge

Challenge

_____

_____

_____

_____

_____

_____

_____

_____

_____

_____

_____

_____

_____

_____

_____

_____

_____

_____

_____

_____

WEEK FOUR:
PURPOSE

"Developing and Dispatching Godly Leaders"

Week 4: PURPOSE

THIS WEEK'S CHALLENGES:

Check below
once completed

☐ Continue Proverbs reading plan

☐ Complete Section2, Lesson 4 in: "A Man Called Jesus" book (pgs. 20-27)

☐ Write personal mission statement

Optional:

☐ Read Chapter 4 in "The Brand Within" and complete attached handout

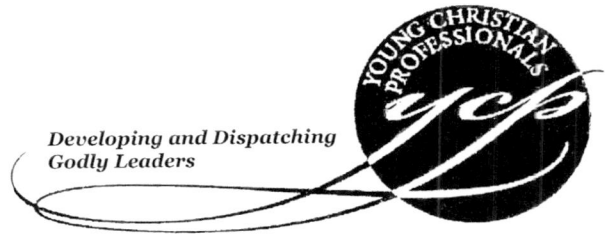

Developing and Dispatching
Godly Leaders

Week 4:
Purpose

Read Psalms 20:4 and Psalms 139:13-16

Finding your purpose in life is one of the most profound moments one has in their life

Your purpose has to be:

• Life long

• Continuous

• Impactful

In one statement, your purpose has to be _____

**Read Proverbs 3:5-6

• Purpose is found by _____

and _____

These 5 letters are an acronym for the things God uses to **"S.H.A.P.E"** you for the purpose He has called you to.

Spiritual Gifts

1Corinthians 12:4-12
Recognizing your spiritual gift or gifts is key in your purpose.

John 4:24
Worshiping God in spirit and in truth includes utilizing the gifts He has given all of us.

Ephesians 4: 4, 11

vs. 4	Your purpose is part of the unity of the Church
vs. 11	Your spiritual gift is also important to the body of Christ

1Peter 4:11
Our ultimate purpose in life is to _____

Heart

Psalm 20:4
God has placed things in our heart that we are naturally drawn to do or are passionate about. That desire should be surrendered to Christ to be used for His will.

Abilities

Matthew 25:1
God will not call you to a purpose if He has not given you the ability to fulfill that purpose.

Personality

Ephesians 4:12
Personality is an "indicator" of your purpose

Experiences

Revelations 12:11
Your experiences are used by God to reach those same people.

WEEK FOUR:
THE BOARDROOM

Week 4:
The Polished Young Man & Woman

- Respect. Never walks between others when they are talking.

- Never views someone's family pictures and say nothing. Always finds something positive to say and is sincere. Silence may be viewed as judgmentalism.

- Never cuts in a line, no matter how tempting.

- Avoids speaking over others at a table.

- Bewares of interrupting people. Wait until people are finished or have a break in their conversations before you interrupt. If you stand at a comfortable distance, they will eventually acknowledge you.

- Respects others religious beliefs. Trust God and pray for them.

- Practices Patience (everywhere). Remember, patience is not just about waiting, but waiting with a good attitude.

- Avoids the trap of borrowing or falling into debt. Stay away from borrowing electronic items from others (players, phones, clippers, headphones, TVs, adapters etc.). If they break while in your possession, guess what?

- Avoids gambling! (and basketball if you have a temper.)

- Is security minded. Don't be a tough guy (or girl), lock your stuff up (for their sake). This helps to avoid finding yourself in a situation.

- Space. If you're in an institutional environment, give your bunkie space. When he/she comes out of the shower, give them time to get themselves together. Or if your bunkie works all day, give them some space when they return. This reduces the tension of living in such small living areas together. Plus, if your bunkie works and lets you watch his/her television, be done before they arrive if you want them to continue extending that courtesy to you.

- Keeps a urinal space or stall between you and other users, if possible.

- Is always courteous. This is not a sign of weakness, but of respect. If you give it, you will get it.

- When somebody greets you, always ask how they are doing as well.

- Cleans up after themselves, despite the temptation to leave their mess as is.

- Loves thy neighbor. In other words, respect the bunk areas. Guide impassioned discussions between friends to the dayroom, especially at night. Some people have to work or go to school.

The Golden Rule:
"Treat others how you would like to be treated!"

PROVERBS READING PLAN

Read a chapter of Proverbs each day of the week that corresponds to the day of the month it is. Write your insights below from a particular verse in that chapter.

Chapter_____Verse_____

Insight: _____

_____

_____

_____

Chapter_____Verse_____

Insight: _____

_____

_____

_____

Chapter_____Verse_____

Insight: _____

_____

_____

_____

Chapter_____Verse_____

Insight: _____

_____

_____

_____

Chapter_____Verse_____

Insight: _____

_____

_____

_____

Chapter_____Verse_____

Insight: _____

_____

_____

_____

Chapter_____Verse_____

Insight: _____

_____

_____

_____

Challenge

Challenge

WEEK FIVE:
YOUR POWER TEAM

"Developing and Dispatching Godly Leaders"

Week 5: YOUR POWER TEAM (Mark 2)

THIS WEEK'S CHALLENGES:

Check below
once completed

☐ Continue Proverbs reading plan

☐ Complete Section 2, Lesson 5 in: "A Man Called Jesus" book

☐ Give something of value to someone you do not know and write about it

Optional:

☐ Read Chapter 5 in "The Brand Within" and complete attached handout

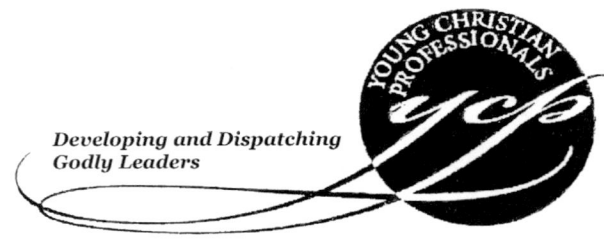

Week 5:
YOUR
POWER TEAM
(Mark 2: 1-5)

Read Mark 2:2

1. What is a Paralytic? –

2. Who is your part of your Power Team/Support system? Who has compassion for you? Who feels your pain?

3. What should we look for in a Power Team?

- (Prov. 1:5) – _____

- (Prov. 8:17, 10:4) –_____

- (Prov. 20:6) – _____

- (Ruth 2: 17) – _____

4. Are you one of the 4 men? Can you be the person that cares for someone else enough to take them where they have be to get God's blessing? (Mark 2:5)

"You don't attract into your life what you want, but you attract who you are."

"Birds of a Feather flock together"

5. Who can be your greatest Power Team member? _____

- John 15:13-14 "Greater love has no man than this, that one lay down his life for his friends. You are my friends if you do what I command you."

- CONCLUSION
- This business/success stuff means nothing if Jesus is not on your team and we have not taken care of the business of our souls.

Mark 8: 36
"What profiteth a man, to gain the whole world and forfeit his own soul?"

WEEK FIVE:
THE BOARDROOM

Week 5:
How to Stay Focused in a Chaotic Environment

1. STUDYING

- When preparing to study, if available, be sure to wear headphones or earbuds whether you have a radio or not. If not, tuck your cord in your shirt or pocket *(the apparent inconvenience of taking them off to ask a question is your first line of defense and will prevent most people from disturbing you).*
- If someone still disturbs you, be polite and answer their questions briefly, and attempt to put headphones back on.
- If they are long-winded, stand up, exchange departing pleasantries, and head toward the restroom. Most people will get the message.
- DO NOT leave an empty chair next to the table you are studying at. This invites visitors to sit down for a "counseling session."
- Hats and/or hoodies *(if your institution permits)* are items that should be worn while studying if the weather permits, as they are extra deterrents to bothering you.
- Study facing a wall *(if your environment is safe enough)*. Your back to the wall is also an inviting posture for interruptions.
- Take notes at events, highlighting key points and principles. Great students take great notes.

2. DESTINATIONS

- The Young Christian Professional avoids wandering aimlessly.
- Wherever you have to go, go. Avoid distracting conversations along the way. Stay on course until you reach your destination.

- If distracted with a conversation for too long, ask the person to walk with you to your destination. If it is important, they will.
- Honor passes early. Most facility policies permit those inside to leave 15 minutes early than pass time.
- If possible, sit in front row seats. Arriving early will likely allow you to hear the speaker/facilitator clearly. *(In society, some seminars cost thousands of dollars to attend. Why spend your money and not receive maximum results? Start good habits now.)*

3. TIME MANAGEMENT

- The Young Christian Professional always uses his time wisely *(even if they are just sitting and thinking)*.
- Minimize and monitor your TV or cellphone use. Practice fasting from them at least once a month. TV's have "programs" for a reason. (Job 31: 1)
- Plan your day the night before. On a scratchpad (or device), write down an itemized list of the things you have to do and need to complete. Scratch off as they are completed. *(This helps build personal integrity by having done what you actually set out to do. It also gives one a sense of accomplishment.)*
- KEEP YOUR WORD. Meet people where you said you would meet. If something more important comes up, still try to meet your prior obligations. If you are not able to, or forget, find the person and tell them your forgot. *(Don't wait until you run into them to tell them. They will appreciate that.)*
- Never go to a computer or typewriter without a plan. Think beforehand, then execute.
- Smell the roses. Spend time with people *(not just people you deem important)*. You don't need to spend hours in conversation, but just checking on people may lift their spirits...and yours!
- If writing, start writing and stop making excuses. You don't get inspired by waiting, you get inspired by doing.

PROVERBS READING PLAN

Read a chapter of Proverbs each day of the week that corresponds to the day of the month it is. Write your insights below from a particular verse in that chapter.

Chapter_____Verse_____

Insight: _____

_____

_____

_____

Chapter_____Verse_____

Insight: _____

_____

_____

_____

Chapter_____Verse_____

Insight: _____

_____

_____

_____

Chapter_____Verse_____

Insight: _____

_____

_____

_____

Chapter_____Verse_____

Insight: _____

_____

_____

_____

Chapter_____Verse_____

Insight: _____

_____

_____

_____

Chapter_____Verse_____

Insight: _____

_____

_____

_____

Challenge

Challenge

_____

_____

_____

_____

_____

_____

_____

_____

_____

_____

_____

_____

_____

_____

_____

_____

_____

_____

_____

WEEK SIX:
TURNING FEAR TO FAITH

"Developing and Dispatching Godly Leaders"

Week 6: **Turning Fear to Faith**

THIS WEEK'S CHALLENGES:

Check below
once completed

☐ Continue Proverbs reading plan

☐ Complete "A Man Called Jesus" book

☐ Read the story of David in one setting (1Samuel, Chapters 16-31), and write an essay about it.

> Optional:
>
> ☐ Read Chapter 6 in "The Brand Within" and complete attached handout

Week 6:
Turning Fear to Faith
(Judges 6)

1. In your own words, what is fear?

2. Don't fear, WHY? Read Psalms 46:1-3 and 2Chron. 20:15.

The battle is not _____.

God is _____ and _____, always ready to

_____ in times of trouble .

3. Fear will cause us to do many things. What are some of them through scripture?

(Mt.14: 22-31) _____

(Mt. 26: 57-58, 68-75) _____

(Judges 6) _____

4. What will help us fight against fear?

(Ps. 27:1) _____

(2Tim 1:6-7) _____

5. Yes, fear will come, but when it does what 2 things should we do? (Ps. 56: 3-4)

TR____ST
PR_____SE

6. Read Heb 11: 1. What is Faith, in your own words?

FAITH- (Heb. 11:1) _____

_____

Faith says in Mk. 10: 27_____

7. Should faith be seen or not? (James 2: 17: Mt. 9:2)

8. How should we live?

(Heb. 2: 4) _____

(2Cor. 5: 7) _____

9. Hebrews 11: 6 says what?

10. What will help us build our faith? (Rom. 10:17 & 2Peter 1: 5-8)

11. What did Jesus Christ do to show He had faith over fear? Use a story out of the Gospels to answer the question.

WEEK SIX:
THE BOARDROOM

Week 6:
Relational Polish

- The gentleman avoids horror movies on early dates. Instead, he goes lighter, with a comedy or drama.

- Keep a clean and tidy car. This is a reflection of you and your thoughts.

- Never mix jewelry at the same time (i.e. a silver chain with gold pendant. Tri-color jewelry is an exception).

- Never stare at a woman, especially if you don't know them. And definitely don't stare through office door windows. Decide if you will knock or not.

- Never disrespect any woman, and respect her even when you are at odds about something. She is somebody's daughter, sister, or mother.

- Likewise, a woman should be respectful to men

- Avoid playing loud rap or rock music on a date.

- Avoids using curse words or vulgar language. This is unbecoming of the young professional.

- Avoid extending your hand first to shake a woman's hands. Pause for her to make the first move (in professional settings, this rule can be relaxed)

- Greet the man first with a handshake when meeting a couple, then greet the woman. Wait for her to extend her hand as well if she wishes to shake your hand.

- Never initiate hugging a woman you don't know or have just met. Learn how to lean in and hug women who are not your wife or partner. Avoid letting her breasts touch you. Make hugs brief and never slide your hands across their body. Also, a one-handed hug from the side is a great, friendly hug.

- Gentlemen, avoid putting your hands in your pockets or pants when speaking with women.

- Never humiliate a woman with "cat calls" or loud flattering comments in public.

- Never joke about a woman's weight or lack of.

- Never hit a woman.

- If a woman says "No," this means no.

- If married, he avoids counseling women alone behind closed doors.

- Unfriends women on social media that cross the line.

- Kindly prevent women from "innocently" touching you.

- Avoid interrupting women who are chatting, especially in the morning (they are catching up and bonding, and you are unlikely to get a favorable response.)

- Always offers to stop at the store for his woman on his way home from work

- Always picks his woman up from the airport no matter what time it is.

- Accompanies his woman to doctor's appointments

- Always remembers his woman's (and her kids) birthdays (especially if he knows the stats of sports figures)

PROVERBS READING PLAN

Read a chapter of Proverbs each day of the week that corresponds to the day of the month it is. Write your insights below from a particular verse in that chapter.

Chapter_____Verse_____

Insight: _____

_____

_____

_____

Chapter_____Verse_____

Insight: _____

_____

_____

_____

Chapter_____Verse_____

Insight: _____

_____

_____

_____

Chapter_____Verse_____

Insight: _____

_____

_____

_____

Chapter_____Verse_____

Insight: _____

_____

_____

_____

Chapter_____Verse_____

Insight: _____

_____

_____

_____

Chapter_____Verse_____

Insight: _____

_____

_____

_____

Challenge

_____

_____

_____

_____

_____

_____

_____

_____

_____

_____

_____

_____

_____

_____

_____

_____

_____

_____

_____

_____

Challenge

WEEK SEVEN:
THE KEYS

"Developing and Dispatching Godly Leaders"

Week 7: THE KEYS

THIS WEEK'S CHALLENGES:

Check below
once completed

☐ Continue Proverbs reading plan

☐ Write your testimony in 2 pages (Write your past, how you came to Christ, and how He has been working in your life since then)

Optional:

☐ Read Chapter 6 in "The Brand Within" and complete attached handout

Week 7:
THE KEYS

Developing and Dispatching Godly Leaders

What is The Blessed Life to you?

I. Hindrances to a Blessed Life

1. **Materialism** - a great or excessive concern with material things as opposed to spiritual or intellectual things

- Why do most people want to be successful? (Ecc. 4: 4)_____

2. **Vices** (Prov. 23: 29-35) - Drinking; drugs; promiscuous sex; gambling; too much food etc)

3. Laziness

Prov. 10: 4   _____

Prov. 10: 26   _____

Prov. 12: 27   _____

Prov. 6: 6-11   _____

II. Weapons for the Blessed life

1. **Saving** - Wealthy and wise people produce this good habit (Prov. 21:20)

- Why is it important to save?_____

2. **Hard Work**

Prov. 10: 4   _____

Prov. 12: 11, 14, 24   _____

Prov. 13: 4   _____

Prov: 13: 11   _____

3. **Diligence - Persevering and painstaking effort**

Prov. 12: 27   _____

Prov. 6: 6-11   _____

4. **A Good Partner**

Prov. 18: 22   _____

Prov. 19:14   _____

Prov 12: 4   _____

5. **Proper Planning**

Prov. 21: 5   _____

Prov. 16: 3 _____

Prov. 24: 27 _____

6. True Humility

Prov. 22: 4 _____

III. Master Keys to a Blessed Life

Matt. 6: 33 _____

and

_____

WEEK SEVEN:
THE BOARDROOM

Week 7
SERVANT LEADERSHIP

(Excerpts taken from "Servant Leadership" by Dr. Jack Schaap)

- Biblical leadership is servant leadership. The servant leader is servant first. In the world, one who stays faithful long enough will eventually rise to the top. In servant leadership, one earns the right to serve. We prove that by proving to whoever asked us to do the job, that they were right in choosing us.

- A servant leader doesn't need a job description. They pick up litter when they see litter. The servant's greatest power is choosing to do work that must be done when nobody else is doing it.

- Attack. When you choose to stand for Christ, you will come under attack. One reason why people don't take a strong stand for Christ is because they don't want to be pointed out as different. They don't realize that taking a stand is part of the turf of success. The person who is making progress and moving forward will automatically stand out.

- A servant leader must know that all that they have was given to them from the Father. Do not jockey for position—because you do not want to be given a leadership position you have not earned.

- A servant leader must know that they were chosen or sent by God and therefore must answer to God. Having this knowledge gives them the boldness and courage because there's no other place to find courage.

- Servant leadership is centered in humility. Those with humility don't deny their power. They just recognize that it passes through them, not from them.

PROVERBS READING PLAN

Read a chapter of Proverbs each day of the week that corresponds to the day of the month it is. Write your insights below from a particular verse in that chapter.

Chapter_____Verse_____

Insight: _____

_____

_____

_____

Chapter_____Verse_____

Insight: _____

_____

_____

_____

Chapter_____Verse_____

Insight: _____

_____

_____

_____

Chapter_____Verse_____

Insight: _____

_____

_____

_____

Chapter_____Verse_____

Insight: _____

_____

_____

_____

Chapter_____Verse_____

Insight: _____

_____

_____

_____

Chapter_____Verse_____

Insight: _____

_____

_____

_____

Challenge

_____

_____

_____

_____

_____

_____

_____

_____

_____

_____

_____

_____

_____

_____

_____

_____

_____

_____

_____

_____

_____

Challenge

_____

_____

_____

_____

_____

_____

_____

_____

_____

_____

_____

_____

_____

_____

_____

_____

_____

_____

_____

_____

_____

_____

WEEK EIGHT:
TRUSTING GOD

"Developing and Dispatching Godly Leaders"

Week 8: TRUSTING GOD
THIS WEEK'S CHALLENGES:

NONE!

CONGRATULATIONS!

Week 8:
TRUSTING GOD

What is Providence?

"The continuing action of God by which HE preserves the creation which He has brought into being (preservation), and guides it to His intended purposes for it (government)."

This means that we are able to live in the assurance that God is present and active in our lives. We're in His care and therefore can face the future confidently knowing that things are not happening by mere chance.

Read Genesis 37: 1-12

1. Do you see anything unusual about verse 15?

We approach the Scriptures as an investigator looking at an old case

2. What are some of the things you should do as an investigator?

3. When Joseph arrived at Shechem, if he didn't see his brothers or the man and returned home, what might have happened?

4. Has there been someone in your life that directed you into a living hell?

Read Genesis 50: 20

5. Why we sometimes go through horrible things: (2Corinthians 1: 3-4)

6. Our response to this trauma: (Matthew 6: 14)

God is in control in our lives, just as He was for Joseph (Romans 8: 28)
"And we know that all things work together for good to them that love God, to them who are the called according to his purpose."

Read Matthew 6: 25-34

WEEK EIGHT:
THE BOARDROOM

Week 8:
THE PROFESSIONAL

1. PUTS CUSTOMER SATISFACTION FIRST - Phil. 2:3

_____

2. STRIVES TO PROVIDE EXCELLENT SERVICE- Titus 2:7-8

_____

3. DOES MORE THAN EXPECTED - Eph. 3: 20

_____

4. DOES WHAT THEY SAY, SAYS WHAT THEY CAN DO - Mt. 5:37

_____

5. COMMUNICATES EFFECTIVELY- Eph. 4: 29

_____

6. FOLLOWS HIGH PRINCIPLES - Psalm 15: 2

_____

7. PRAISES THEIR PEERS NOT THEMSELVES - Prov. 27: 2

_____

8. IS COURTEOUS AND HAS GOOD MANNERS- Titus 3: 2

_____

9. SAYS THANK YOU - 1Thess. 5: 18

_____

10. KEEPS A SMILE AND A GREAT ATTITUDE - Prov. 15: 30

_____

Congratulations on completing the Y.C.P. Course and becoming a consummate professional!

To help you stay on track throughout your journey, remember these tips:

1. Value all people and relationships

2. Continue to stay humble by seeing others more important than yourselves

3. Treat all people with respect

4. Follow through on what you start

5. Add value to the lives of all you meet!

Made in the USA
Columbia, SC
13 May 2025

57724180R00049